the iceworker sings
and other poems

Bilingual Press/Editorial Bilingüe

General Editor
Gary D. Keller

Managing Editor
Karen S. Van Hooft

Associate Editors
Karen M. Akins
Barbara H. Firoozye

Assistant Editor
Linda St. George Thurston

Editorial Board
Juan Goytisolo
Francisco Jiménez
Eduardo Rivera
Mario Vargas Llosa

Address:
Bilingual Press
Hispanic Research Center
Arizona State University
P.O. Box 872702
Tempe, Arizona 85287-2702
(480) 965-3867

the iceworker sings

and other poems

ANDRÉS MONTOYA

Bilingual Press/Editorial Bilingüe
Tempe, Arizona

ISBN 0–927534–86–X

Library of Congress Cataloging-in-Publication Data

Montoya, Andrés M., 1968–
    The iceworker sings and other poems / Andrés Montoya.
      p.   cm.
    ISBN 0–927534–86–X (alk. paper)
    1. Hispanic Americans—Poetry. I. Title.
    PS3563.054588I28   1999
    811'.54—dc21   99–12111
                                         CIP

Acknowledgments

These poems were originally published in the following journals:

In the Grove: "the ice worker sings"; *The Santa Clara Review:* "truly"; *Flies, Cockroaches, and Poets:* "the escape," "letter to antonio tomachek aragón," "locura," and "sight"; *Bilingual Review/Revista Bilingüe:* "in brown america."

I would like to thank my teachers Philip Levine, Garret Hongo, T. R. Hummer, Corrine Hales, and Juan Felipe Herrera.

For Luci Saez Montoya, the two sticks of her affection,
the empty tomb and the parting of clouds.

". . . Even so, come quickly."

—St. John the Beloved

contents

iii

iv

i

in search of aztlán

i came looking for aztlán
but couldn't find it
it had been hidden with names
like fresno   parlier   earlimart

i came asking questions of my family
but my family could only remember
how the last paycheck
was swallowed mysteriously
by the valley's hot air

sight

felix watched
    from across the street
        as the city
        official
    sank a thermometer
   deep
      into the sick
       smile
     of blood
       and flesh.

the brown body
      laid
    quietly,
       discreet in its somber absence
         of light,
       telling when last
           the blood ran warm.

the dusty dead
      end road
    began to whisper
     rumors
    about the murdered
        man's life:
      he was a gangster
    who got what he got
        which is what he deserved,
           or
      he was the boy
        barely a man
          who slung rocks
        with a smile
          in front
             of the boarded-up hous

or maybe
he was no one
in particular, just a man
on his way to the public phone
to call his woman.

felix watched
but didn't really
see.
he kept thinking
how the cracks
in the sidewalk
reminded him
of the cracks
in the silent slab
outside
the welfare office,
his children saying over and over
with laughter and smiles like song,
"step on a crack, break your mama's back,"
and he felt
bitter
about the angry glare
of the dead man's
body.

the ice worker sings

it didn't matter to him that it was only seasonal
or that he had no choice but the graveyard shift;
a job in the ice plant in the hot fresno summer
was as close as he'd get to heaven.
or at least, this is what he thought.

he liked this job cause they let him alone.
here, everyone wore ear plugs
and he was left in a room
by himself to stack blocks
of ice into rows of crystal perfection,
rows and rows, a huge army
of petrified water standing at attention.
he found himself marching back and forth
singing songs he never knew he loved.
sometimes he would sing rock
or blues or even a classical tune
he'd heard on a bad radio commercial.
but, mostly, he would steal the beats
and put in his own words about life,
about love, about dying.
this is how he became a poet
parting ways with the sad ocean
of ordinary speech. he sang loud
and he liked it. no one ever told him
to shut up, or that he couldn't carry a tune.
he enjoyed seeing song
spring from between his lips
in the white breath of the cold room.

he found he could forget everything
while he sang among the ice:
the house that kept shedding shingles,
the mad dogging eyes that followed him
to work, and his cowardice under the yellow street lamps

while he knelt on the road of potholes and gravel and dust
begging the moon to release him from his fear of everything.
but here he sang, and his army of ice
to him were warriors from tula, big
square warriors, sympathetic to the orders
of their general, which, of course, was him.
they laughed when he laughed
and cried when he cried.
only here, he never cried.
he didn't have to.

at home, his mother slept with the windows open
in hope a breeze would finally blow.
at home, they didn't have refrigeration.
at home, even the walls were hot.
on breaks he would sit outside
on the bench to smoke and drink coffee.
here he would pray for his mother,
pray for angels to come carrying machine-
guns and flamethrowers
to keep watch over her.
he would pray for wind
so that she, like him, might escape
the hell of fresno in the summer.

and when the break was over
he would go back to the ice
and give life to his army,
he would go back to the ice
                    and sing.

the ice worker in love

he is in love.
friday nights before work
he sees his woman.
they are not married
and she doesn't know
that he loves her.

he tells her
her hair is like water
and her skin smells of dew.
and she tells him
it'll still cost the eighty bucks
for the three hours
in the crusty motel
that smells of smoke.

he doesn't know her real name.
he thinks it is sofía.
one day she will tell him the truth,
that her name is alexandra,
that her family calls her alex,
and he will feel a little betrayed.

sometimes they smoke weed or crack,
sometimes they do lines of crank.
always, though, they lie naked
next to each other when they are finished,
sweaty and both feeling a little guilty.
they only do it once. he never asks for a second.
and they are content to listen to each other's breathing.
he likes the way she sounds so alive,
the rise and fall of her breath like pain and pleasure.

the conversation is the same every time.
do you ever think of God? she asks.

sometimes, he says. this is why he loves her:
she reads him stories from the Bible
found in the dresser and he is fascinated.
he likes the one about the people in the desert
following a cloud in the day and a pillar of fire in the night,
and he wishes that he had something to follow,
"something to lead me out of this crapshoot life," he thinks.
sometimes she tells him about a man murdered

forgiving everyone, even his own killers.
this is when she cries, and he feels he too should cry,
that he must cry for the man murdered who forgives,
only he doesn't know how, yet.
he only knows that he likes to hear
her stories, that there is something good in her voice,
he only knows that he can smell life in her breath
behind the stale stench of the room's desire.

denial

i am limping again
across the huge cracks
in the concrete city
i call home. it's wet,
rain falling for days,
car fumes turning purple
in the night.
light bouncing
off puddles created
by a boy's
despair
as he kicks it
with his friends
in front of the shop-and-go
by radio park, on the corner
of clinton and first streets,
where they killed louie,
where lion puts his mark
in beautiful graffiti growling
in reds and yellows
as you drive by the bus
stops and telephone poles
and fences or whatever else
he can tag his hope on.

i'm tripping again
and the flesh lying on the bones
of my left leg is accusing me
of crimes that, truly, i'm guilty of,
and i keep wanting to wander
around this town of gangsters
and prostitutes, family and tears,
and tell the clouds in the sky
that keep spitting insults at me
as if they were spitting rain

wet like the dew drawing dawn,
it isn't easy to ask for forgiveness,
it isn't easy to love justice
and judgment like an ax
splitting open the hard
heart of my life.

i keep running into things i know:
a car busted on the side of the road
like the bruised back of a boy,
a car ownerless
and sad without sorrow,
soaked and shining
in everything we despise.
i keep running into myself:
hungry and disgusted
at the scars on my back,
trying to shoot the pain
into the thin blue line
running up my arm,
while my friend who
sells herself keeps saying,
"look how loco you are, mijo."
i keep running into people
who got no place
except a room
with a fridge
and its dingy
dim light
making
even the cockroaches
look romantic.

—something ain't right—
i keep saying
but can never put my finger on it.
when i run into the woman

with the ratted red hair
and the yellow-green
teeth like a pool of water rotting,
the woman standing outside
city hall in the rain
yelling at the city's rulers,
"repent! repent!
the revolution is at hand!
Christ is at hand.
judgment is after you, boys,
like a rake in a yard full of leaves.
repent! repent!"
i think just like everybody else:
the woman's insane.

in brown america

in brown america
life keeps going and going and going
and the grapes keep growing and growing
and the anglos keep owning.

don't make this a race thing
they keep telling me.
whi te on br own bro wn on wh ite
lets just get along,
said a white waitress at denny's
who laughed and said,
besides, they can kiss my racist white booty,
because she thought i was one of her,
                    my pale skin becoming red with
anger
        and
                embarrassment.

at night,
here in fresno,
when the air is hot
and still,
i can hear
the brown and black
whores
calling my name,
knowing that the state
paid me today
and my wife is in
bakersfield
visiting
relatives.

1981

the night always scared you
ever since they shot efraín in the face,
leaving him to bleed to death on the long dirt road
between the peach orchard and grape field.
you wanted someone to hold you the night you heard,
someone to protect you, but when your mother came
it didn't stop the sky from warning you:
your turn was coming. you were eight then.

and at thirteen
you pretended to be the friend of death.
you boxed your cousins
who never pulled their punches
when making you a man. they told you
to always scar your enemy on the face,
a deep gash down the cheek,
because this was a sign
to everyone of your locura.
and you believed them: they were alive
in the streets that wanted them dead.

so that night in 1981, when you walked alone
through the flats, midnight, a knife in your pocket
and num-chucks caressing the forearm
hidden in your jacket, you pretended
to be a man. but the wind whined
and the bushes blew.
the shadows became the demons
that always wanted to eat you.
you didn't cry, no, not then,
but your heart was ready to break
and your eyes flicked around
and a thin line of sweat
gathered at your upper lip's edge.
you forced yourself to walk slower,

a mean strut to deny the darkness
that was ready to leap on you.
were you ready for the boys
who beat your brother dead?

there was the sound of the road
and the cars grumbling along.
a dog kept barking on one
of the lonely streets,
but all you remember
is breathing like an animal
as the ground before you
came up under your feet
as if the world were spinning
in slow motion beneath you.

the front of your house
seemed haunted in a fog
that was only in your mind.
the car was there, crippled
and green on the curb.
the skin of the garage
was peeling and the porch light
had been stolen, leaving the grass black
like a square hole. were you afraid
of being swallowed?

you went inside
and watched tv alone.
your mother waiting
for the alarm, your sister
breathing deeply
and your brother
already gone.
you went inside
and watched tv alone,
as if nothing was happening,
as if all this was natural.

locura

and where, raza, are our heroes?
         the heroes of aztlán?

what became of that great nation we were going to build?
where did all the warriors go with their sharpened knives
                and loaded rifles?

everyday i walk through the cracking streets smelling despair like a rose.
i ride on buses freshly laced with the stench of some borracho's vomit
and there are bones and more bones stacking up around me,
murdered by pipes and cops, knives and guns, or just the evil glare
of some rich gava. and not the viejitos sipping tea, or the lovers loving
behind the bushes in the park can make me smile or laugh or see
some glimmer of hope in this crazy cosa called life
         cause i can't get out, the streets keep returning to me the same,
         always the same
              like a bad dream, and i have come to the conclusion
that this is how it was meant to be: death in my pocket and insanity
the limp that keeps dragging me down. a tattoo teardrop falling from
    my eyes.
         i can't sing anymore.
              no whistle pushes forth
                   from between my lips.
i'm gettin ready to bust out loco, and no one hears when i'm yelling

"i gotta go, gotta get outta here!"

so i   smile now   with a cuete tucked in the back of my baggies
and a .40 in my right hand, imagining myself some kind of chulo
cholo, or some other form of vato loco or just another ciclón
waiting to put some little chump stepping up punk down

and then when i'm doing the tecato shuffle, or the borracho bump,
dying coughing in that cockroach motel they found louie in
i'll cry and i'll cry and i'll   cry later   like the tattoo says,
and no one will be the wiser, not my mom working the graveyard
or my girl who looks like her mother, that little girl with my abuelita's
name, who will probably die younger than me
and it all comes down to the fact
i've lived the life of a coward,
a slave, i never had the guts
to explode, really explode, like cuauhtemoc or zapata,
suicide style so my gente can live like gente with honor.

the escape

it doesn't matter that his chin is too long
or that the left side of his upper lip
is being pulled into his nose
      by a hair of skin.

it doesn't matter that he never asked
to the prom the girl who smelled
of rosemary and dirt wet
      from the rain.

it doesn't matter, the regrets for quitting
school at 16 for the job at PDM steel,
or that the union's been bought
since '76, or that since he started
callousing his hands on the cool
face of metal, he's lived his life daily
asking like a child about to be beat,
"i wonder if they'll lay me off today."

he's sixty now and never been married
and it doesn't matter that he's lonely,
that he left the woman of his dreams,
the hitchhiker he never picked up,
somewhere on the 99 south of selma
      in 1972.

it doesn't matter that today he woke again
hating everything without knowing it.

it doesn't matter that he's drunk again

it doesn't matter that he swerved
to miss the kids playing on the corner
of the prostitutes, that he plowed
his pontiac into the waiting side

of someone's car, that watching
were witnesses staring from the mouth
of the sorry street littered with fast food
bags and the fake ghosts of hope and life
teasing everybody.

it only matters, now, at the end of the long day,
that their are still two blocks left before he
can begin his journey up the walk to the waiting
cushions of the soft sofa staring out
     from the crumbling house.

fresno, august '92

the brown boy lies dead   spit slipping red
from his mouth   in bubbles   to the dry   cracked dust
         of the ground   sucking it up   like the juice
                 of a stepped-on orange.

the alley

for rangel, 1985

jesse's dead.
he only wanted
to take himself out,
but the cops came
and shot him
27 times.

        *

his sister
of the huge
owl-like eyes
saw the whole thing.
not a drop of juice fell
from his quiet body
without the angry
contempt of her
breath.

        *

his mother
came screaming,
but jesse never moved.
the cops shook hands, giving
congratulations all around.
they'd survived well.
jesse's father tore
at the dark skin
of an old tree
looking for
answers.
nothing.

ii

question

can you hear it now
life in the middle of it all
this field of dust and poison
and pain like a perfectly orchestrated song
whelping out its measures of silence?

being born

i was born in 1978 from asphalt
and the beat-up bumpers of chevys

      on fourth and vine
on sanjo's south side. they keep
      telling me it was raining
and the lighting was licking the streets
up and down as if the world was a cheap motel
room with cockroaches propped up on the pillows.

they keep saying it was a sign,
the rain and its lightning,
of my darkness.
      they say
i was meant for evil.

      they say
what else can come
from a syphilitic john
and his saturday night
      whore.

but it ain't so.
      i keep waiting
for the clouds to bust out
in lights. i keep waiting to hear
a trumpet so fine
that the man miles
will bow his knee.

i keep waiting to hear
the Man say,
      "good goin' tommy
            you all right."

they say i was born
from a witches womb.

but i'm tellin' ya
        i was born in 1978
bowing broken on a chevy's bumper
        my knees digging into asphalt and glass
and a puddle of gunk
        on fourth and vine
                on sanjo's south side,
        my chest heaving a lifetime into the air,
                the moonless night.

i was born in 1978
        sobbing Christ from my lips.

some days

the other day

>   when the sun was yawning
>   into the beautiful bruise
>   of the horizon

the other day

>   after the brown boy
>   caught the cop's drift
>   in a satanic bullet

the other day

>   after the cops told the boy's wife—
>   who accused them with her sobs
>   —shut up or die   whore!

Christ wept in a church
through the eyes
of a chubby boy

silence

it wounds me, this silence. even
the tears have been abandoned.

and though i collect the salt
from all the eyes, tasting them,

filing each according to its purity
of sadness, this too is forgotten.

forgotten.

the dead girl's laugh on a saturday
afternoon, pierced and pondered by
a stray bullet's incredible insight.

forgotten.

rené who loved the smell of his son's
skin, remembering his folds of flesh
in the holes of his nostrils, just before
the cops came with their .357 smiles.

and i keep waiting for the screams.

screams for the man mumbling
imagining himself embedded
in the perfect life of a rose.

screams for the woman wailing
in the back room of a dying apartment,
her life living itself out of the bowl of a glass pipe.

i keep waiting for the screams.
screams for the dead, the dying, the decayed.
but there is only the mute moth eating away at everything.

it wounds me, this silence.
and though my wounds, like coins, are nothing,
though i lose them and find them again,
it is still true, this silence wounds us all.

you see,

this is the silence of the dead man dancing
singing forth the crimes of the rich.
but who hears you dead man? who listens
to the truth falling muffled from your mouth?

you see,

this is the silence of Christ beaten blue
and black on the scorching streets
of the city, Christ mistaken for a gangster
or thug or just another mojado moving
in on the precious property of "providence."

and everyone, everyone, is washing
their hands in the silence of these sins.
there is not one innocent. no, not one.

the ice worker considers
mercy and grace

i will make no confessions here.
can't you see i've been bathing in blood?

i am not on my knees and there is no screen between us
and you are not a priest, are you?

once, i told my crimes to a poet
like a sinner sighing into the moonlight,
and he looked at me with his eyes
that wound wild circles in the sky
—the left one in outer space
and the right one twirling
round and round—eyes that opened wider
and crazier than they already were when the stink
of my savagery found its way from my poem
to his nose, and he asked in his proud wisdom,
"do your words stutter because of your horrific essence?
    find it boy, embrace the truth and the truth will set you free."
as if somehow he had me, as if this was the enlightenment i needed.

once, i became proud of my sins,
a warrior taking off his shirt to share
his scars at the corner church like a bar,
telling the story of each curve in a cut,
each gorge of mangled flesh a story
i pretended to be sorry about, but each time,
in each story, though evil i was,
somehow i became the hero.

but i will not give you, here,
the address of my sins,
i won't give you the phone number
on a piece of paper folded
for you to slip neatly in your wallet.

you see, someone once told me,
as i explained the crimes of the villa doreen
apartments, as if they were the sins of someone else,
   he cried,
  "he's gonna burn! that son of a she-dog whore!"
and he was screaming at me with his pious pocked cheek.

and it was true. i deserved to die.
i deserved to burn. so i do not desire
the complicity of poets or the humble trumpet
 of my pride.

      *

this is the naked truth:
Christ came walking up blackstone avenue
and i dragged him into an alley
and spit in his face. he didn't say anything
 and it pissed me off.
i shoved a beanie of thorns onto the thin skin
of his head and laughed. he began to bleed
but he said nothing, so i spit again.
my friends, the preachers and cops
said, "nail him! nail him!"
    so we yanked off his beard.

the whole city came to look
   so we set him on the alley's
     trash-can throne.
   all of us applauded, even you.

channel 30 news came with their cameras
and we raised him up, as if he were a snake
in the desert, on two sticks. we raised
him up like a flag, a banner,
as if we were soldiers. we laughed,
me and the professors from the college,
we laughed and his blood kept dripping

from his hands and feet and side and head
onto our heads, but instead of shame
we played craps for his sweatshirt.

you see, this is the truth.
you see, i don't have anywhere
        to hide from this.

no confessional of wood will do.
    only blood bathes.

i don't want any of this
        to be true. but what can cover me?
        the sycamores have forgotten my name
        and the willows have stopped their weeping.
        even the dogs of my neighbors have learned how to accuse me.
i cannot hide from this man or the sag of his body. they say he is a god,
        but i keep asking, "what keeps a god nailed to sticks?"

and there is only the whisper like an echo falling from rocks,
        "love keeps him nailed there. love"

the ice worker finds hope
in cold storage

he's bending
broken, knees burrowing
into the chipped pieces
of ice littering the floor.

it is hope
plucking tears
from his terrified
eyelids.

hope exposing
the savage hieroglyphics
spattering his belly
and back, spelling out
a life that should never
have been lived.

he's bending broken, knees
burrowing into the chipped
pieces of ice littering the floor,

hope exposing everything
          —as if for the first time—
he should weep for,

his sorrow leaping
from his mouth

into the stale freeze
of the refrigerated room,

his breath
a white fog
of camphor.

the ice worker explains to the judge why he is not guilty of loitering in the great parks of the city

i find myself, sometimes, sitting on the curbs
of huge city streets, comparing my legs
to potholes and my breath to dust
whipped up by colorful cars passing.
people pass me by, too, as if i was not there
as if i was not a man with ratted black hair
and dickies dying on my legs
as if i wasn't a man mumbling
"kentucky" and "weep"
over and over again.

i find myself composing poems
and reciting them to walls
and to the children
that hold them up
with their crippled
screams of paint.

once, on a friday
in the rain
i went around
the downtown mall
laying my hands on trees
and the doorposts of stores
saying prayers, asking for the blessing
of Christ to come down like a jackhammer
breaking us all to pieces.
but they didn't want to hear it,
they kept calling the cops.

no one wants to hear it.
but that's ok; i have skinny dogs

following me, who pray with their
hoarse howls. they moan.
there are cats in the pack, too,
and an occasional rat marching
with me and never a grumble
about the incredible lack of cheese.

we sleep on the dirt patches of sorrow
and we drink the water of murder
and we eat the invisible bread
offered to us by the city
from its busted coffer of love.

they won't let me work
anymore; the bosses always claim
the dogs and the cats and the rats
are a public nuisance
getting in the way of progress.
but when i ask them
to provide for the poor
jobs instead of songs
food instead of votes
and hope instead of accusations,
they look at me
as if i was a crazy man
changing the subject
to the face of the sorrow
that scars the hole in the back
of their heads.

i'm just an ice worker
who likes his job
and wants to gather
people in parks,
who wants to gather
children on street corners
and pray:

our Father who art in heaven
hallowed be Thy name . . .

but people laugh at the moaning trees
and the moaning dogs.
people laugh at the moaning
        children.

i'm just an ice worker
who wants to write poems
of praise using words
like "kentucky" and "weep"
to the huge Creator
of the sky.

but no one ever hears it.
when i go to city hall
and read the poetry of their lies
they say, "this is not the place for poems."

so i find myself singing to alleys and trash cans,
to ants and the crushed peach of their affection.
all i have is the park and the trees and the swings
to sing to about the imminent return of justice.

the rains have left and ernesto is dead

for trejo

the rains have left
and the air is hot this day.
in between
the rows of vines
sparrows are feeding
on a dog and his worms.

there is no breeze
to rustle the grape leaves
or to cool the dry
pocked faces of prostitutes
around the villa motel.
there is only this season
and this night
to breed anger
in the empty stomachs of children.

a car passes on the road in front of my porch
and whips dust in swirls and again
the smell of sulfur
catches my nose by surprise.
so long, it seems, i've been
in this valley off the 99,
watching the children play in this dust,
watching mothers cry out
to God for justice for peace for death,
watching the honda civics passing by, passing through,
never stopping on this side, this scary side violent side,
this side of misspent anger.

yes, it's warm
and swamp coolers only
make me sweat more. from my porch

i can see three campesinos walking
into town, covered in dust, and i wonder
if their children will be deformed,
or maybe they will die soon,
leaving the fields to no one
but the farmers.
the sparrows have been frightened
from the dog by the three,
but they will return
to pick from his flesh
what they can.

brittle green teeth

I.

i am only a man. this is what my legs
keep telling me. "andrés, you are only a man.
why do you keep looking to the sky that way
as if you were going see something other
than the mournful face of your life?"
and it's true. i'm just clay.
dust and spit and breath
wheezing my way through.
my slaughtered history
haunts me. am i different from my
grandfather? he abandoned
his brother's forehead to the snow,
a bullet begging blood
to drip purple to the ground
on some mountain in new mexico.

II.

it is dark and i pretend to hide.
how do you keep finding me?
i am naked; please go
away. why do you
keep coming after me
like this? don't you see
the scars on my back? my
life made them. my breath
smells. it gags me. don't
you see how i keep loving
this place? i make treaties
with cockroaches. the counters
are theirs and the bed is mine.
i keep forgetting to bathe

and my eyes keep finding
their way to madness. where else
can i go? i never understood
how blood bathes, but only the truth is true:
a tree planted on a skeletal hill
and a man murdered. a man flying
into the sky only to return. where else can i go?
who else can make beautiful song sing
from between my brittle green teeth?

the ice worker speaks of endings

the moon has turned into an accusing street lamp
and i keep hearing the loud breath of helicopters

and the incessant cough of guns going off everywhere—
pow! pow! pow!—as if silence had been taken hostage

somewhere to the north, silence and peace tied up
and gagged in a pantry filled with rich man's food.

don't ask me to prove things to you. there's no time.
don't ask me to paint pretty pictures or draw diagrams

explaining to you how we got here. just breathe
and you'll smell the truth. feel the flesh of rage,

rotting, coughing, and dying, and there's nothin' you can do
to stop this apocalyptic ball of wax from unraveling. nothin'.

i keep sittin' here thinking sometimes of the woman i wanted
to love, the land i wanted to retrieve. i'm sittin' here under

the cool moon's glare reciting Bible verses to the tree
in front of my house, to the bermuda grass, to the side-

walk and street and wires that crisscross this neighbor-
hood. you see, i'm waiting for the end of the world

and the earth is full of violence and the hand of God is calling
"cover yourself! cover yourself! i love you so much. cover!"

but there are only cars and trees and the touch of a lover for a minute.
there are only wires and grass and now, here and now,

     the clouds are opening into light.

iii

for you

here i am
i have rocks
tattooed
on my smile

this is all
i can give you
take them

letter to sarah

the wind comes claiming again
its right of way through the valley

and i'm sitting in the field of vines
where as a child i chased wasps.

my large nostrils are full of dust
and the smell of ripe grapes.

i am explaining you to the peach moon
that hangs there low and listening,

but my mouth merely hangs open
and i find i don't know enough

to explain anything. i have only
a memory resting in my gut like

a tear already fallen from the face.

after looking for che in the lines and rhymes of a poem, the young man decides to write the crazy gypsy

for luis omar salinas

omar, last night when the moon threatened to expose me
i jumped into a river, into a boat, untying my steed
with the speed of a thief, thanking God my getaway had begun.
i can't tell you the names of the trees that passed or the colors,
but i tell you the frogs howled like hounds and dared me
from my spot. i said to myself, "i'll find omar
where the poor gather to speak baseball and politics.
he'll be there, i know, talking the philosophy of a whisper,
interpreting the dream of a widow, quick with a tear
for a boy smelling of ditch water."
omar, i've been doing the tango all day
looking for you among sleepless mothers and drinking men, searching
with the smile of a madman. i want to ask you about the whistle
of a line, a gava's evil glare, about the family
of a woman who died in one of my poems.
omar, i need to confess. when pachuco children growl
in their stomachs, i wish my poetry was a rifle to take aim.
i don't have time to be a gypsy or an aztec, i'm just chicano, an indian
who sees life swallowed up in a dream and wants to explode.
i know you'll see the anger of a peacock in my eyes
and understand. i know you'll say, joaquín, do what you have to do.
omar, i need to swim in your river of words,
your giddy interpretations of despair, your hope for the sadness
of our days. i want to give my gratitude on a plate
with beans and rice, with a laugh, a beer, thankful to talk to you at last,
discussing streets of the angry barrio.

landscapes of sadness:
a letter to the artist from his son

for my father, who taught me justice
is always worth fighting and dying for

I.

here, where first i felt the sting of the wasp's
whisper in these fallow fields,

where wind whips dust into moaning
visions of the earth's ancient murder
by the first couple seeking God's demise,

here, there is sadness.

this is perhaps fowler, or del rey, or parlier.
it doesn't matter. the story and the sadness
are the same in these towns found clinging
to the 99's long leg.

this is the story you already know:

a boy named césar found, now, only in the fading photos
of his mother's scrapbook, in the memories conjured
        by a moonless night's glare.

he use to come with his left eye leaning into the sickness
that threatened us all, and his right eye lazy, limping
        far behind his gaze.

he use to come with his bat and his glove, calling out
the names of ballpark heroes, "garvey, cey, valenzuela,"
as if at any moment they would move from the shadows
        and shout along with his voice.

he use to come shouting his poetry,
"garvey, cey, valenzuela! garvey, cey, valenzuela!"
over and over again, until we all heeded his piper's call
and came with our gloves to the makeshift diamond
behind the fourth street church.

but these memories, like photos, fade.
and now i know only that he died,
murdered slowly, like the earth before him,
cancer creeping through his bone's marrow.
i know only that he was executed one year
in the grape field's gas chamber.

II.

i came here looking for you, an image, a ghost,
something i could crawl into and imitate.

i came searching the streets of cities
and the long lonely roads of the country,
but i found only sadness breathing
itself from the trees, calling up
from the canal's cold water, seeping
into your daughter's heart, horrified
as she held césar's balding head hung low.

did she understand it all?
did she know the farmers knew of the poison's
power to slowly plow a life under? that death
and decay would follow as they added field unto field
until they alone lived wealthy in the land? did she
know, like adam and eve under the trees, the killers hid
from the face of God, under their tangled vines of money,
sewing together grape leaves to mask their naked
aggression, grape leaves of legislation to convince
their consciences that it was merely satanic songs
sung by a little man and his leftist movement

instead of Christ calling,

where are you?   what have you done?

III.

i came searching for you but found only your sadness
brushing up against the canvas of my life. sadness

carving creases into your hands and face, when as a child you turned
trays, your back battling the sun beating down like a board.

i, too, found this valley heat harsh, sunstroke striking me
into a haze so clear i never wanted to understand anything again.

but i kept coming against it, this life, and somehow i could smell you.
you had been there before me, cutting, forging a way through
the rows of field dust and the same concrete reality that comes
presenting itself again and again and again. this is
what i found.

IV.

i want to tell you, the anguished truth of sorrow demands
    from us courage. you taught me that.

i want to tell you
    i believe in consequences for all of this,
    i believe in judgment.

    i believe glory will come on the clouds
    and the mourners, the murdered, the earth,
    the groans coming from the womb of grief
    will all be born again into joy, born again into life.

i want to tell you, father, i believe in the Resurrection.

letter to antonio tomachek aragón

antonio: the night tonight, with its sad anger
hanging around like the dark clouds
of madness, reminds me of the drum beating
from your heart into the mouth of the heavens.
what am i to say? leonard peltier sits under
the same moon as us tonight—shadow sticks
striping his face—injustice weeps into the sad breath
of everything, a maya warrior dies on the streets of fresno
never realizing who he was, and the whitehouse remains
the whitehouse. my muscles have left me.
you already know this. and yet i still want
to fight. i am in love with justice, though
sometimes my foot slips on the rocks.
i am in love with humanity, though
sometimes i punch myself in the face.
what will all this come to? today,
across from the house of my mother,
i saw four boys surround another boy.
i just sat and watched. four boys
surrounding another boy. at first
i thought, this must be child's play.
but they acted as men. men and crazy
and in love with power. they acted like cops.
what spirit is this? what locura haunts
these streets winding down from conquest?
what was it that paralyzed me to my seat?
fear? cowardice? curiosity sick in the solitude
of my heart? or was it despair? so much to do
and nowhere to start. this must be where dying begins.
tonight, i want to hear the drum beating from your heart.
i tell you it is Christ who has put it there. does this offend you?
i keep praying that the warriors will rise from the earth
like corn strong on the stock. i keep praying for sanity.
       oh, God, have mercy . . . .
i get angry, carnal. i hate what has happened. i use to hate

because my mom couldn't pay the bills, because poverty
became the only treasure she ever owned. but now i hate
it that we all feel helpless to do anything about it.
our leaders have become clowns
who frown at any talk of fighting. they are whores.
God, have mercy on them. i want to hear the beating drum
of your heart because it reminds me not everyone hates justice,
not everyone hates truth, not everyone hates Love. your carnal, andrés.

a letter to kb

kb: tonight the sky in fresno was different shades
of blue. dusk and clouds splitting into two huge arms
like a man reaching to God through sadness, through the stars,
past the moon, as if lifting his arms in praise and thanksgiving.
i wonder if you saw the same old man floating up there.
i am remembering san francisco. you, me, and your sister sitting
in a cafe. the coffee was bad. do you remember? you pretended
to be a mechanic that day. your catholic cheek is what i see still
and the fear that rested on your forehead like a butterfly waving
its wings ready for flight. san francisco. that city always reminded me
of plastic: shiny and freshly pulled from the mold and painted
with sea salt and sheen. i had no memory in that city. in that city
i had amnesia.

here, the memories rise up like anger, like teeth sharp
and sinister. they rise up like the lover you can't bear to leave:
i found my brother, one day, behind a door, arms spread wide
like Christ on the cross, laid out on the floor over a pile of colorful
clothes ready for wash, the sad slashes at his wrists weeping
into the stench of stale cigarette smoke and poverty that held captive
that room, his eyes deep dark wells wet and begging for the logic of death.
goya would have painted this had he had to live with us
in that crumbling house in fresno, in the flats of melody park.
i don't know why, but i love this image, i love this city. if hope
cannot be found here, then where? hope. frisco was never
like that for me. what memories do your hands hold of that city?
what is it that you find beautiful there? perhaps you could paint
for me an image in glass, colored in truth and hope.

have you heard from roque lately? has he taught you any new words?
you know, sometimes i think he is so full of crap that i could
close my ears to him forever. but it is his passion, his love
that has infected me. this must have come from God.
he painted justice on the lips of humanity, and struggle
on the forehead. it was love he sketched on the cheeks
and hope he brushed into the eyes. he didn't know it

but it was a picture he painted of our Christ, alive
and extending a hand of mercy, ready to give justice
to the poor. but isn't it crazy, sister, that we keep thinking
of Christ as a thief? what is it that he would take from us?
the love we have for our own legs? sadness? suicide? self-hate?

when i was a kid, i betrayed, like judas, my own brother. i love him
even now, his face smooth and jaw square. his eyes were two
huge apples alive in the sun. he smelled of ditch water
and weeds. he was beautiful, that boy. he wanted us
to be brothers forever, to be beat into song under a starry
starry night. but i was in love with power more than i loved
him and i left him on the ground weeping
more at the sight of my back than the memory
of my fists. and when i saw him on the floor, his wrists split
open at the heart, i was angry. i wanted to beat him. i hated his
powerlessness and i wept not for him or for my mother
who would have to bear all of this, but for myself, for in his blood
i saw my life running away in lies and I couldn't stand him.

i am ashamed.   what a fool i was. what a scared little boy
i was. he was Christ that day and i held a hammer
and a handful of nails. this is what i hope Christ takes from me.
why is it that we keep believing the propaganda
that God is in love with injustice, or that he is dead,
or, at the very least disinterested in the pain and fear
and love we feel? Christ is alive, and my cheeks
want to touch his, my pores are waiting for him,
and my nose can't wait to feel the heat and wet
of his breath. does this sound strange to you?

i am wondering what you look like in the valley.
what does your name sound like there? does it still smell
of grass green and wet under a sky of morning?
i pray that in your heart will be found hope as huge
as the sky that waits for the coming of clouds. i pray
that you are smiling. i pray joy will be found singing
from your ocean-like eyes. thinking of you, sister: andrés.

hope

for my mother

the wind whispers itself from the trees
and again i am remembering your hands

raised to the sky in defiant praise—defying
a life that kept saying "no! no! death is all

you have!" but your hands were raised
in a sigh of victory, Christ on your lips,

and life was placed on your beautiful
forehead, and the glory of God shone

from your face. this is the inheritance
i desire: a hope, a strength from the blood

of the Murdered Man, a murdered king, raised
to the right hand of God. hope in the two sticks

of salvation placed on the skull's hill
so many years ago. how can i repay

you for this gift? for this image
of strength sounding itself in the incense

of praise before the throne of God?
on clouds of glory He comes, and our hope

is not disappointed. He is waiting at the edge
of the sky, and we are saved.

lágrimas

yes, it's true. your eyes do not deceive you.
this man doesn't breathe. this man
that touched my shoulder years ago,
whose sister smells of el fil,
this man at my feet is dead.

see? dead. in the chest.
those three holes in red.
see how the shirt is striped now
in a haze of splatter and spider leg
streams to the ground, flowering
from those three holes?
Go ahead. feel them,
feel how sticky, like warm honey.
let flesh flow warm
over your fingers, smell gunpowder
and the faint sting of sea salt
floating up in blood fumes and soul.

i never knew him, either. not really.
actually, it wouldn't be a lie if i told you
we were once friends who watched
our lives crawl across counters
on the backs of cockroaches.
me and this man lying at my feet.
it would even be true if i said, once
when fresno's sun was angry, always angry,
we swam shirtless in ditch water,
mud squishing through our toes,
and never once did he say a thing
about the purple-black welts on my back.
me and this man lying at my feet.
but that was when i was a boy.
i am a man now.

i never knew him. not really,
because he became a man in the mists of car fumes
and me in the poisoned clouds of field dust
and it wasn't me that killed him, not here
at this playground with the trees pushing
at wind, with it's dry green grass.
you see, i killed him long ago in the field
across from the flats, the melody park colonia,
in that field of fruitless dirt clods and the night
was strong with stars and a navy blue sparkle,
the night smell came on with exhaust
and slaughtered peaches. i killed him there
after he beat me with a sharp chain
and i don't even remember now why,
but he beat me and i was the child
that i was, sticking him
with a buck knife to the belly
until his body fell limp
to the dirt and i slept.
this is when i killed him.

no, this is not my doing. dogs did this,
this real thing, a man lying at my feet,
blood pooling at my too-large boots.
i did not do this, this was not me,
this was done by boys barely men
growling from the gut, but it was not me
that made him fall here. i tell you
he must have died all alone
while i slept at home and he ate
here at the playground when the boys
came to talk papas and eddie,
yes i will give him a name now
a name like my name, a slave name,
eddie galaviz said to get the hell back
and they shot him, like that, and laughed,
running into the streets of the barrio.
this is how this man died, how eddie died.

i can't even imagine it. and it was not me
but i still can't seem to cry for you, eddie,
i don't hate you anymore like that night
i threw the knife and it didn't stick
that night you beat me with the chain,
and i wonder if it would be a lie if i said i loved you,
but i still can't seem to feel for your flesh lying limp
here,
no roses will fall from my eyes to bury you,
to soak up your blood. this will be left to dirt.

you're dead. so many dead, eddie,
and your name could be jesse or leonard
or zapata or cuauhtemoc and you'd still be dead.
shall i cry for you? should i do this for you?
i will give my tears to your murderers, the boys
who know death as just another day.
i will cry for those whose hope crawled
away like your life, for your own
brother in the pinta and your own sister
of the packing shed, for my brothers
and sisters, i will cry for the barrios
and los files, for my mother who's known only work
and worthless men, my mother who lives.
i will cry as if from the womb of the earth
to the heavens, to God, to have mercy
on la raza and los pobres.
i will cry for resistance and struggle, for your song
like the song of our murdered ancestors
joining in the marrow of bones
fire running through veins.

luciana: this is how i see you

how will i remember you, grandma?
    will it be your name, luciana, that i recall
        on nights when the forgetful remember
    everything?
           luciana: beautiful
        like the wind winding whispers
           through the arms of the trees.
   luciana: my sister carries your name
      and she wears your earrings
         and her birth will forever carry
           your heart
               beating boldly for the truth.
how will i remember you, abuelita?
    will it be in the kitchen
        tortillas on the comal
           eggs frying in the pan
              and a song of praise
                  pouring forth from your lips?
or perhaps
    it will be your face, a bruised petal of forgiveness
      as you told me your story
        on a saturday afternoon
        in dixon,
        how grandpa came for you
      smelling of sheep and whores, how your
        grandmother
was old and tired and begging for the cool sheet of a warm bed
    to lie down and forget her life, how she sold you or traded you
        dragging you away from the dolls
           to stand before the priest
              and become a woman at
              twelve.
      or maybe
        i will remember you
    hobbling into the grocery store,

the nylons gathering at the back of your knees
           like wrinkled skin,
                 like survival.
will i remember your hands, your beautiful hands,
     two measures of tender masa
           you use to lay on the faces of all your children?
will i remember your prayers prayed,
           the powerful breath of your hope
                 forging a way for us all in this madness?

i tell you grandma, this is how i see you:
     you are dancing, your straight leg is bending and your hair
        is waving wild
     as beautiful laughter like song strums from your mouth into the sky,
     and your eyes, your eyes are catching the shine of the Son,
     like two huge apples begging notice on the tree, and you are shouting
     with your smile, "hallelujah! hallelujah!" and all the angels
        are dancing and
     laughing with you, and Jesus is saying, "i love you so much, mija."
     and you are saying, "mi amor, mi amor," like a beautiful sigh.

iv

birth

coming forth from this earth, this dirt
our flesh climbing into form, into existence
the Creator with breath made mud to breathe.

star struck

sometimes these walls ask me,
"were you never happy, love boy?"

●

i would step out
into the night
into the alley
where the ants
savored the crushed
anguish of a peach

and the road was nothing
but dirt with worn tracks
of tires, two arms reaching
to the place i had always wanted
to go, but never knew how to get to.
the night, to me, always
smelled sweet with grapes
and stung the back of my nose
with ditch-water breath and dust.

from my house at the edge of town
across from the high school football field
across from the dying field of vines, i walked
into the darkness. it was here
that i learned to love
as the sky opened
like a huge howl of lights
and the sounds of frogs
and crickets and birds baptized
my ears into hearing.

i would walk through the rows
of fruit, my feet always hesitating,

content with the despair
of the dying city of progress,
my feet sinking into dirt clods
and sand seeping into my shoes,
into my socks, as if in conspiracy
with the potholes of my street
or with the cracked walls of my room.

but my heart dragged us on
to the bank of the ditch
that oversaw the drowning
of an old dining room chair,
where the rim of a wheel
jutted defiantly out
from the wall of mud and stone,
and the abandoned trash
of grape wood and kitchen bags
became homes to blue-bellied lizards
and widows.

there i would sit
pulling tobacco from my pocket,
putting pinches of sweet leaf
into my mouth, watering,
and i would lay back in the weeds
while the water rolled by,
my feet caressing the cool kiss
of the ditch. and there i would breathe,
really breathe deep,
as if sucking the stars
into my chest, as if i was taking
life forever into my soul.

there i would sit
and sometimes weep,
not because i was a boy
so alone, but because

in the blue-black bruise
of my life, in the middle
of steel and fruit ready to rot,
i could find the cold love
of earth beneath my back
and God smiling,
making promises
from the sky.

the sky is only something

the cars pass.
there are buildings
and a girl screaming
sobs like song
from the starving hole
of her heart,

and though i want to weep with her
my eyes are dry and only my chest
understands that this is about blindness.

my chest: the heart begging to break forth
into ballads for my love. love begging

to break through from behind the bones
        of my face, my cheeks and my forehead.

i drive and drive and drive, not knowing what corner
this is i'm rounding. i can't seem to pray. at least

not a deep contemplative-meditative-mystic type prayer.

i can barely whisper past my moaning throat, "O God have mercy!
        Jesus, save me!"

i pass the corner again of the child begging to hold on
        to anything with the crippled calligraphy of spray paint,
        poems he imagines will save his soul.

i pass that corner again of childhood where the boy
        begs to meet the Maker through the long black tube
                of an ugly glass pipe.

everything in me wants to jump upon him
and anoint him with my tears. would he be surprised
to see me after so long?

"O God, what manner of love is this . . . ?
i cannot find you. find me. without you
the sky is only something hanging
        over a potholed street."

but i can't cry. something tearless
bellows from my belly and i keep driving.

altar call

tonight you go back
to the edge of that town
where the grass smelled sweet
and the sky, in silence, sang.

it seems, now, in your nostalgia
to have lost the weekend
the varela boys hunted
you through the alleys
and the bushes of the park,
it has lost the days of sun
and sulfur in the fields of dirt
and sand and the farmer barking
orders into the stale breath of heat
as you stumbled from vine
to vine going nowhere.

tonight, this is a town of silence,
a town of wind when dusk
grabs the peach moon
in its purple passion
and sings praise in spite
of the cracks in the concrete road.
you come here hoping to meet Christ
at the abandoned football field
where once your father played,
hoping to meet your Savior
as if on a hill of skulls.

tonight, you have found your altar
in this town of shadows
and whispers so loud under
the wide mouth of heaven.
tomorrow comes quickly
and your eyes sigh,
melting into stars.

contemplations
from concrete:
nine movements

#1 scar

i was born from concrete
and sea salt. my hands
are tree bark and my mouth
spews the stench of the sewer.
you are so beautiful
i am afraid to speak about it.
how will you love asphalt
        cracks and dust
smiling up at you?

#2 fear

i don't know anything of love.
i know about the bus schedule,
how poems are written on the backs
of seats like a law accusing me
of my own pathetic limp.

i know how to stare a man in the eyes
just to say, "i'm ready for you, punk!"

or how death looks
lying on the street
under a white white sheet.

i tried to love once
but ended up punching
everybody.

what can you
do for me? see?
even my questions
come out wrong.

your breath is too sweet;
        go away.

#3 voice

"come
lie with me

the gunshots
will still be there
after you have learned
the lesson of my kiss

rest with me
here on the floor

i am singing to you

isn't it more beautiful
than the thrown rod
of a chevy
stumbling lost
through the neighborhood

come
let me
pronounce
your name"

#4 tell me

you know me
too well.
the map
of my scars
you have already
charted.

tell me your name

so i can
whisper it,

weeping,

with my eyes
closed.

#5 voice II

"come
be born
from my heart
exploding
from the split
skin of my side

my forehead
is a garden
calling
your lips

my hands want
to weep on you

can you hear
the whisper
through my feet
over the whelping
of your neighbor's
dog   the whisper
through my feet
as i walk the cracked
cement path
to your door

can you
hear
the whisper
through
my
feet
calling,
'lover! lover!'

      between us
these are the only wounds"

#6 education

i am learning
      the braille

            of your breath
    your word

   your voice
          leaping
      up from the page
         into my mouth

#7 rest

i sit in my room.
the light is blind
and the shades
asleep. i am quiet.
this is hard for me.
i always want to talk.

you are across the room
whispering. your breath
is wet and warm against
                my face.

#8 revelation

the patient ocean
of your eyes
pounds open
my heart's
cold door

bringing
fire.

#9 prayer

you are hot.
i can barely
breathe.
you smell
good.

truly

i would give you a star. a multitude.
perhaps
           if i were a romantic
             i would say:

from the sky i have stolen stones of fire
and strung them together on a tight
invisible string of fishing line.
i have brought them to lace
the shiny skin of your neck,
your wrists, brought them to wrap
your ankles, plant them one at a time,
carefully, in each of the nails of your toes,
starlight lighting the dirt before your feet.

but this would be a lie.
                they were already yours. the stars.
             a lie.
        your feet never needed their light.

what then?
the sun? the moon?   yours.
                  maybe that single berry
                  begging notice on the vine?

but even this has fallen
from your breath.

i can offer you
a piece of flesh
fallen from my bones.
another. and another.
another. rotten and smelling.

the bones,
      a bit yellow,
            too, are yours.

i give you
this image:

if you brought fire
                at the end of a stick,
or maybe just a hot coal,
          a burning ember,
and touched my lips
burning away to the gums
          and gums to the skull
             and skull to the soul to the spirit,
       i would finally sing you,
truly sing you, on my knees, my forehead leading the way . . . love.

fresno night

a jazz trumpet finds the lips of someone unsuspecting and the stars
   find huge caves

      of light to hide in. i am left with the quiet power
of the heat and a horn echoing off the cages of concrete
      and cars and the cold metal madness of this city.

      off in the distance, perhaps on tulare ave,
a cop's corrupt hand is finding its way around
      the neck of a boy suspected of being illegal

      and in the park, radio park, lovers laugh
at the imagined future of their unnamed children,
      at the stories they'll tell as grandparents

      still savoring the breath of each other's skin.
in this city i sit waiting for the end of the world.
      the neighbors of noah are everywhere

      and a strange sky has come staggering in.
i am not holy or noble or righteous, but i still,
      from my crippled mouth call, "Christ, Christ!

      let your blood bathe me and not night's nasty
glare, let love's power bind peace around the neck
      of my soul, and i will stand confident, clinging

      to the Cross when the storm's scream comes
stinging at the heels of your saints. oh, Lord have mercy!"
      i am not unusual, you see. i am in love, in love

      with a girl from the sea who sleeps with her head
in the valley. i cry and laugh and live in the dust of the earth.
      i am born, bought with blood into the Spirit, but

still this flesh is of clay, of dust, of death.
but hope holds my heart: the word made flesh, laid down
    and picked up again to the right hand of glory.

    here in this city i sit, the trumpet's trembling song
fading away like an adulterous man, and i am left with car horns
    and gunshots and shouts and smells of grapes

    just about to rot on the vine, surrounded by wasps
whispering lies and mothers weeping for children brainwashed
    with insanity, and i am determined to know nothing

    but Christ and him crucified.